copy 2

S0-BFD-271

Are You My Bird?

by Marybeth Mataya
Illustrated by Matthew Williams

Content Consultant:
Gerald Brecke
Doctor of Veterinary Medicine

magic
wagon

Text by Marybeth Mataya
Illustrations by Matthew Williams
Edited by Jill Sherman
Interior layout and design by Emily Love
Cover design by Emily Love

Library of Congress Cataloging-in-Publication Data
Mataya, Marybeth.
Are you my bird? / by Marybeth Mataya ; illustrated by Matthew Williams ; content consultant, Gerald Brecke.
     p. cm. — (Are you my pet?)
Includes index.
ISBN 978-1-60270-241-7
1. Cage birds—Juvenile literature. I. Williams, Matthew, 1971- ill. II. Title.
SF461.35.M38 2009
636.6'8—dc22

                              2008003633

Note to Parents/Guardian:
This book can help your child become a kind, responsible bird owner. Even so, a child will not be able to handle all the responsibilities of having a pet, so we are glad that you will oversee the responsibilities. If you are going to allow your child to take the bird out of its cage to let it fly, you should have an expert trim its wings. Then you can let it out in a small, closed room. Always keep an uncaged bird in sight. Leave the cage open so the bird can return to it on its own, or gently urge it to perch on your finger and carry it back.

Table of Contents

Is a Bird the Right Pet for Me?   4
What Kind of Bird Would Be Best?   6
What Does My Bird Need?   13
Where Should I Put the Cage?   14
What Else Should Be in the Cage?   17
What Should I Feed My Bird?   18
How Do I Get to Know My Bird?   20
How Do I Keep My Bird Safe?   24
How Do I Stay Safe?   28
Words to Know   30
Further Reading   31
On the Web   31
Index   32

Is a Bird the Right Pet for Me?

Do you like the sound of chirping and singing? Do you want a colorful pet? Do you like to spend time talking to someone? A bird may be the right pet for you!

When choosing your bird, have all family members spend time with it. Some people are allergic to birds.

Pet Fact:
Many birds like to be part of a flock. Your bird's flock includes you!

What Kind of Bird Would Be Best?

Zebra finches are colorful. The males are great singers. Finches like to be with other finches. But, they do not like to be handled much. They live for about four to five years.

Canaries are in the finch family, too. Most people think of yellow canaries but there are many colors of these birds.

Canaries do not like to be around other canaries. They also do not like to be handled often. Canaries live for about ten to fifteen years.

Budgerigars, or budgies, are parakeets. They are friendly. Most budgies are green and yellow. And most like to be held. They like to whistle and chirp. Budgies live for about six years.

Cockatiels are smart and friendly with people. They are known for the long feathers on the tops of their heads, called a crest. With training, males can usually learn to say a few words. They love to whistle, too. Cockatiels live for about five years.

Lovebirds have a fun name. But, they are not always nice to children. They live for about eight years.

Parrots, conures, and macaws do not make good pets for kids. Most are too large. They bite, and they are loud. They can live for more than twenty years.

LOVE BIRDS

Pet Fact:

Having a wild bird as a pet is against the law. Make sure that a human raised your pet.

What Does My Bird Need?

A wire cage makes a good home for a pet bird. The cage should be as big as possible. Birds need to stretch their wings. They also like to hop and fly a bit.

The more birds you have, the bigger the cage must be. Place paper on the cage floor. Change the paper every day.

Pet Fact:
Finches and canaries like wide cages. Cockatiels and parakeets prefer tall cages.

Where Should I Put the Cage?

Too much sun can overheat your bird. Find a place out of the sun in a well-lit room. Keep the cage away from windows and doors. Chilly breezes can make your bird sick.

The cage needs to be off the floor and away from dogs and cats. Keep it out of the kitchen, or anywhere else with strong smells and gases.

Pet Fact:
Fumes from candles, cleaners, paints, air fresheners, and Christmas trees are not good for birds. Teflon pans can also make fumes that can harm your bird.

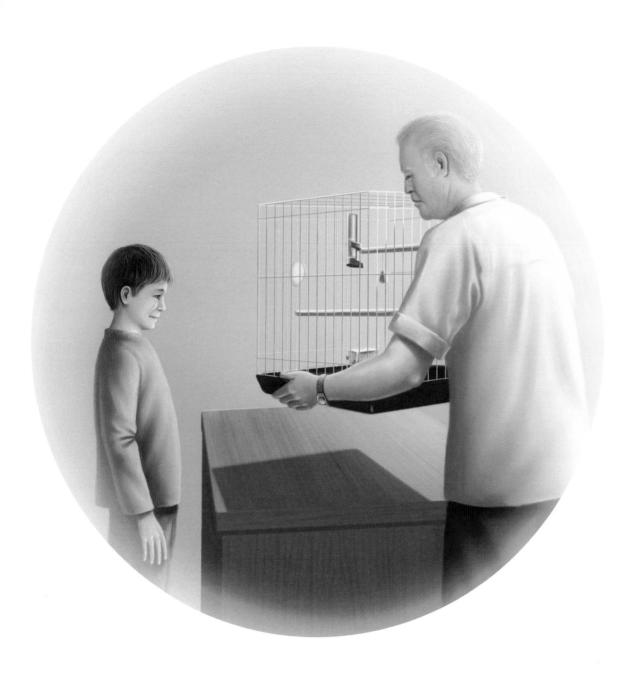

15

What Else Should Be in the Cage?

Birds need perches, or places to sit and rest. Wooden sticks make good perches. Give your bird different sized perches. Place them high and low. Place one next to the food dish and water bottle.

Birds also need toys to exercise and stay healthy. Bells, ladders, swings, and rings are fun. Birds love bath time. Give your bird a shallow dish of water to splash in for an hour.

What Should I Feed My Bird?

Birds like many different kinds of foods. Feed your bird pellets twice a day. Different kinds of birds eat different pellets. Buy the correct type of pellets for your bird.

Birds need to have fresh water all the time. Hang the food and water containers from the side of the cage. This will keep droppings from falling into them. Clean out the old food every day.

Pet Fact:

Not all seeds or leaves are good for birds. Do not feed your bird avocado pits, cherry pits, rhubarb leaves, or apple seeds.

How Do I Get to Know My Bird?

Let your bird get used to its new home. At night, have an adult cover your bird's cage with a sheet. In the morning, uncover the cage. Sit nearby and talk quietly to your bird. Play soft music for it.

Later, hand it a seed, a fruit slice, or a vegetable. Wash the treats before you give them to your bird. Let the bird get used to having treats from you.

21

In a few days, lean your finger lightly against your bird's lower chest. If it steps up, it trusts you. Do not worry if your bird does not come to you. If that happens, try again the next day.

When your bird comes to you, open your palm. Let your bird rest in your hand. Always be gentle with your bird. Never hit or squeeze your bird.

When you are done holding your bird, urge it onto a perch. Lightly pet or scratch your bird's head and neck.

Pet Fact:

If your bird bows its head to you, it wants you to pet it.

How Do I Keep My Bird Safe?

Birds need exercise. It is best not to let your bird out of its cage for the first few months. When it is time, ask an adult to show you how to safely let your bird out of the cage.

Your bird needs to know and trust you. If your bird stretches out its neck and body or squawks, it is mad or scared. Quietly back away.

Pet Fact:
Fear can make your bird sick. Do not to scare your bird or let other pets scare it.

25

Help an adult clean the cage once a week. If your bird is less active, has murky eyes, or has dull feathers, it is sick. Call a veterinarian or ask for advice.

Pet Fact:
Birds like to groom themselves. They use their beaks to comb their feathers.

How Do I Stay Safe?

Do not stick your fingers in your bird's cage. It may bite them. If your bird acts strangely, do not bother it. Tell an adult and bring it to your veterinarian.

Pet Fact:
Birds are very interesting. There are many different types of birds. Find out as much as you can about your bird!

Words to Know

allergic—to have a bad reaction from being around something.

droppings—animal poop.

flock—a family group of animals.

groom—to clean oneself to stay healthy.

murky—foggy or having a dull color.

pellet—a hard bit of mashed up food.

veterinarian—an animal doctor.

warble—to sing with trills and many sounds.

Further Reading

Evans, Mark. *Birds: A Practical Guide to Caring for Your Birds.* New York: DK Children, 2001.

Fusz, Ellen. *Cockatiels.* Neptune City, NJ: TFH Publications, 2006.

Mazorling, Tom. *Parakeets.* Neptune City, NJ: TFH Publications, 2007.

Mousaki, Nikki. *Canaries.* Neptune City, NJ: TFH Publications, 2008.

Mousaki, Nikki. *Quick & Easy Zebra Finch Care.* Neptune City, NJ: TFH Publications, 2004.

On the Web

To learn more about birds, visit ABDO Publishing Company on the World Wide Web at **www.abdopublishing.com**. Web sites about birds are featured on our Book Links page. These links are routinely monitored and updated to provide the most current information available.

Index

A
allergies 4

B
bathing 17
biting 10, 28
budgerigar 9

C
cage 13, 14, 17, 18, 20,
    24, 27, 28
canary 6, 13
chirping 4, 9
cleanup 13, 18, 27
cockatiel 9, 13
color 4, 6, 9
conure 10

E
exercise 17, 24

F
fear 24
finch 6, 13
flock 4
flying 13
food 17, 18
fumes 14

G
grooming 27

H
handling 6, 9, 20, 23, 24

L
life span 6, 9, 10
lovebird 10

M
macaw 10

P
parakeet 9, 13
parrot 10
perch 17, 23

S
safety 14, 24, 28
sickness 14, 17, 24, 27,
    28
singing 4, 6
stretching 13, 24

T
talking 4, 9
toys 17
training 9
treats 20

V
veterinarian 27, 28

W
water 17, 18
whistling 9
wild birds 10